Identifying Training Needs

The Competent Trainer's Toolkit Series
by David G. Reay

Identifying Training Needs is the fourth 'tool' in the series. The first — Understanding the Training Function — stands outside the training cycle. The rest, including this book, deal with the cycle stage by stage, from planning your initial strategy right through to evaluating the contribution training makes to the prosperity of your organization.

All these books can be used on training courses or as aids to self-development.

Identifying Training Needs

Finding out what people need to know and why

DAVID G REAY

Kogan Page Ltd, London
Nichols Publishing Company,
New Jersey

Published in association with OTSU LIMITED

First published in 1994
Reprinted 1995

Kogan Page Limited
120 Pentonville Road
London N1 9JN

Published in the United States of America by Nichols Publishing, PO Box 6036, East Brunswick, New Jersey 08816

British Library Cataloguing in Publication Data

A CIP record for this book is available from the British Library.

ISBN (UK) 0 7494 1285 2
ISBN (US) 0-89397-427-7

Typeset by BookEns Ltd, Baldock, Herts
Printed and bound in Great Britain by
Biddles Ltd, Guildford and King's Lynn

Contents

Acknowledgements

This series is to a large extent based on OTSU's experiences during the past decade. Because of this, so many people have been involved in its formulation, it would be impossible to name them all. However, there are a number of people without whose help this series would not have seen the light of day.

I would like therefore to give my sincere thanks to Paul Leach for his constant support with writing, Adrian Spooner for his editing skill, Aidan Lynn for setting the series in motion, Jill Sharpe and Kathleen Gibson for design and desk-top publishing, Dorothy Reay and Amanda Froggatt for proof-reading and finally Dolores Black at Kogan Page who didn't mind flexible deadlines.

Introduction

At some time in every trainer's career, they will be required to carry out, or arrange to have carried out, a training needs analysis, or TNA.

However, it is not only trainers who are asked to find out the training needs which exist in an organization. There are organizations where training is a sub-function of personnel, and there is no dedicated trainer as such. These organizations will need to ask themselves about their training needs, and the task of getting someone to do it will fall to . . . who knows? A senior personnel officer?

This book will help non-trainers to understand what goes into a TNA: what drives it, where it leads, what's involved. However, because training needs analysis falls primarily in the remit of a training group or department, my primary audience for this book is trainers. In short, trainer or not: this book will reveal to you what goes into a successful training needs analysis.

Together with my team in my organization, I have been privileged to visit many companies in Europe and America to explore their training needs. As a result I have learnt not only that a structured approach is the only proven consistently successful way of conducting a TNA, but also that a structured approach comes as something of a surprise to many of our hosts.

I'm often assured that, 'There's nothing to a TNA. You simply ask "what training do you think you need?" Our people tell us and we give them what they ask for.'

On the surface this simple approach has much to recommend it:

- the end-users of the training are approached
- the desired training is implemented quickly.

But . . .

Yes, there's always a 'but', and in this case it is a large one. What if the workers ask for training *x, y and z,* but they really need training *a, b and c* — and they would have asked for it, too, if they'd known about it, but they didn't.

A structured TNA is based on a balanced view of the organization's needs, the people's needs and the nature of the problems which are being addressed.

The structured approach which is described in this book has been developed as a result of carrying out TNAs with a range of organizations over a period of ten years. I make no claims that this is the only approach possible or that the methods suggested here cannot be improved upon. The only claim I make is that the process works and if you need to change it to meet your organization's needs, then it provides a sound base on which to build your own method.

The approach suggested here focuses on what people produce and achieve rather than what they do. Because of this, it can encompass and implement the precepts of continuous improvement and the need for value-added activities.

The Toyota production system has carried out research which shows that in a business:

- 65 per cent of all activity is wasted
- 30 per cent is necessary, but adds no value
- 5 per cent of all activity adds value.

Given the statistics, a training needs analysis which failed to take account of the value-added factor would risk providing training which would serve only to make the 65 per cent wasted activity a little less arduous and time-consuming.

So what is *Identifying Training Needs* all about?

Identifying Training Needs is all about asking the right questions and then making sense of the answers.

The right questions are those which will provide the basic information the training department needs to enable employees to meet the business needs. As you saw on the last page, there is much scope to improve performance, so the questions have to be pretty shrewd.

The answers you get can easily get out of hand if the questions are in any way vague or misleading. Even accurately targeted, simply-phrased questions will yield a great variety of answers ranging from the predictable to the amazing, from the boring to the absolutely fascinating.

Making sense of these answers is a skilled and disciplined task, calling for focus, clarity and simplicity at all times.

If this sounds challenging, well, don't be alarmed. This book is designed to take you through the whole process of questions, answers, interpretations and recommendation step-by-step, so that you will be able to undertake a TNA on your own or with your team and achieve optimum effect.

Objectives

By the time you have completed this book, you will be able to:
- identify who the customer is when you're preparing your TNA
- express clearly what different parties expect to get from your TNA
- design an effective TNA programme
- obtain and analyse all relevant data
- prepare and write an effective report with recommendations to best meet the needs of the customer.

Training and Development Lead Body Competences

A Brief Summary

Many trainers and training managers in the UK are actively seeking professional vocational qualifications, through the growing National Vocational Qualifications route. And this book and series can help you to achieve them. There are competences at level 3 and level 4 of the NVQ in Training and Development for which you will be able to use this book as part of your portfolio of evidence.

To make it easier for you to include the assignments in this book in your portfolio of evidence, I have prepared, on the following page, a matrix which matches a list of assignments which appear in this book and the competences which appear in the TDLB NVQ book at levels 3 and 4. Simply tick off the numbered assignments as you do them. Then, when you've completed this book, you can include the book itself together with any supporting documents you may create as you work through it in your NVQ portfolio. This simple matching technique will allow your NVQ assessor to easily locate your evidence and match it against the relevant criteria.

While no one assignment fulfils a whole element of competence, each assignment goes towards meeting performance criteria outlined in the elements shown. It follows that this book will make a significant contribution to your portfolio as a whole. Other books in this series will match other criteria in the TDLB list of elements.

Assignment at end of chapter	The Assignment Counts as Evidence Towards these Elements							
1	A111	A112	A121	A131				
2	A111	A112	A122	A123	A124	B131		
3	A111	A112	A123	A124	A131			
4	A131							
5	A131							
6	A121	A132						
7	A112	A121	A123	A124				
8	A111	A112	A121	A122	A123	A124	A132	A133

A111   Review an organization's strategic aims and objectives
A112   Specify an organization's human resource requirements
A121   Identify the current contribution of training and development to an
           organization
A122   Identify the potential contribution of training and development to
           organization development
A123   Determine organisational aims and objectives for training and development
A124   Gain commitment for the contribution of training and development to an
           organization
A131   Collect information from organization's training and development needs
           analysis
A132   Analysis information on organization's training and development needs
A133   Specify organizational training and development needs

Overview

The structured TNA model I propose has eight discrete steps; the book will mirror this by having eight chapters, as follows.

Chapter 1 — Identify the Customer

The eight-step structured approach to training needs analysis is customer-orientated, and the first step has to be finding out who you're providing the TNA for. While you may think that this is obvious, Chapter 1 will demonstrate common misconceptions and how to avoid them. Since the customer is the ultimate point of reference and needs to be closely involved in many of the following steps, accurately identifying the customer is crucial. Identifying the wrong customer can get you into deep trouble.

Chapter 2 — Clarify the Expectations

There are a number of key questions to ask of your customer — questions which need to be answered if you are to stand a chance of meeting your customer's needs. Chapter 2 addresses each question in turn, explaining why it is important and giving guidance to answers you may commonly expect to receive.

Chapter 3 — Design the Training Needs Programme

Among the key issues to be addressed as you're designing a TNA are the resources you've got available, the timescale you have to work within, and the methods you'll use. Chapter 3 looks at all these issues, and gives guidelines to which methods are appropriate to which situations within an organization.

Chapter 4 — Arrange Access to Data

Many a TNA has floundered because it became impossible to ask the right questions at the right time. It's a fact of life that there are often channels to be gone through and protocols to observe. This chapter explains the whys and the hows of arranging access to data.

Chapter 5 — Collect the Data

In view of the planning you've done, collecting the data should be straightforward. Chapter 5 explains how to monitor your data collection and how to avoid distractions and cope with variances from your plan.

Chapter 6 — Make Sense of the Findings

The focus in this chapter is the identification of relevant material. A needs analysis will generate a lot of information and sifting what you need from what you don't is crucial.

You should also bear in mind the form in which you need to present your data so that other people can get the information they need out of it.

Chapter 7 — Write a Draft Report

This chapter allows you to create a structure which will be suitable for your report. It also focuses on your recommendations, stressing the need for all your proposed solutions to take account of your organization's situation and its culture.

Chapter 8 — Produce and Distribute Final Report with Recommendations

Your final report should be the basis for actions to be taken. Consequently, there may be some negotiation between yourself and your customer as the draft is worked into its final form — negotiations which will allow you to present your report so that it will have optimum effect.

Where to Start

A structured training needs analysis is an iterative process.

I've never been in favour of using jargon to display knowledge, or to exclude people, or simply for its own sake, but in this instance, an iterative process is the best description of what actually happens in a good TNA.

A TNA starts with a problem — maybe a real crisis, maybe just an area where there is room for improvement — and returns to that problem at the end. All the time the chief point of reference of the TNA is that problem and how to solve it. The customer commissions the TNA because they want to achieve something; there is always a desired outcome, and the recommendations made at the end of the TNA should allow that outcome to be realized.

Once the outcome is achieved, of course, the situation changes. There will be new areas where improvements can take place, and a new TNA should be instigated to allow these improvements to occur.

Where to Finish

I recently completed a TNA for a very large motoring organization. The recommendations I made at the end of it came in 12 separate parts, only one of which related directly to training. The other 11 concerned changes to personnel structures, pay and other related matters.

It is quite acceptable for a TNA to conclude that there is no training solution to the problem being addressed. I would counsel against your assuming that there must be a training solution to every problem, because to do so will prejudge the outcome of the analysis and can cause problems.

To prepare a training solution to a non-training problem is to invite disaster, because your solution will fail and your credibility as an analyst will be damaged. So will your organization's faith in your ability to provide training appropriate to the organization's needs. Instead, focus on identifying and describing acceptable, practicable solutions to the situation you're addressing. Bring out the training solutions where appropriate, and highlight other solutions where training won't work.

Remember that it's the customer's needs which drive your training needs analysis — and you should focus on them throughout.

Chapter 1

Identify the Customer

This chapter is relatively short and deals primarily with one specific issue: who is your customer?

It is vital that you thoroughly identify your customer, their representatives and their needs for your TNA to be successful. By the time you've finished this chapter, you'll be able to:

- list and apply the criteria which will enable you to identify your customer

- explain the importance of identifying your customer's representatives as well as your customer.

This will put you in a strong position to clarify their needs, and we address this point in depth in Chapter 2.

Customers

As a trainer, you are constantly providing a wide range of services which benefit a wide variety of people in different ways. In one way or another, all of these can be considered your 'customers' when it comes to your training provision:

- **the board and senior managers** who steer and develop the business and who know what the business needs are. Your training helps them meet those needs

- **Line managers and departmental heads** who, in many cases, commission specific items of training from you to meet their specific needs

- • **Trainees** and other people who gain knowledge and skills as a direct result of your training provision

- • **Stakeholders in the business** who do well when the business does well, so your training contributes to everyone's success.

So who is your customer?
Look at the list of potential customers and ask yourself which group or groups are likely to contain your customers for a TNA. Write them in the box below.

In our experience, customers for TNAs tend to be found among board members and senior managers, and departmental heads.

We arrive at this conclusion because of the two main criteria we applied to identify the customers ownership and payment.

Ownership

The person who has ownership of the TNA is the person who will take your results away and implement them or ignore them, as they choose. Usually this same person has ownership of the problem which the TNA is addressing. It is also likely that someone, somewhere will be holding that person responsible for finding a solution. So, you will have to find out from the owner exactly what performance is required of them.

Payment

We cannot comment on the internal market arrangements which exist in your organization. But it is clear that every TNA has to be paid for somehow or other. In some organizations, the commission to carry out a TNA carries with it a fixed budget, literally paid from one account into another. In others, the trainers and the customer may need to negotiate the amount of time and resources they will have to commit to the TNA, and the customer will have the authority to approve. But the person who pays or who authorizes the use of resources should be regarded as the customer.

Customers Who Identify Themselves

Trainers are practical people, and all this talk of 'identifying the customer' may have conflicted with your experience of reality. For many trainers, the phone rings and a voice simply says, 'We need a TNA; come and see me' — and straight away you're into a supplier-customer relationship. We counsel caution. It could be that the caller is in fact a customer — but only if they satisfy the criteria of ownership and payment. Otherwise, they are not customers. And the request? Of course, you should listen to what it is that is being asked of you, and you may be able to help. But if you end up in a situation where:

· you are sorting out a problem for a person who has no responsibility for that problem, and who will be unable to effect any proposed solution

- you divert resources to a problem without proper authority to do so

— then you're sailing right into trouble. You should only undertake TNAs for bonafide customers, no matter who asks you to.

But what if the customer is the board of directors? Who will you actually deal with? Write your answer in here.

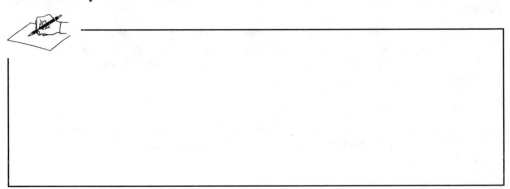

The chances are that you'll deal with a representative of the board with full power and authority to accept ownership of your TNA on behalf of the board, and to pay for it.

Dealing With Representatives

The first step when working with representatives is to find out if they have the power and authority to accept ownership of your TNA. The answer you receive has major implications for the next stage in the process. Much of the responsibility for keeping the TNA on track will be yours. As you'll see in the next chapter, you need to get into your head the ideas which motivate and drive your customer. However, good working relations with representatives are essential.

It is also essential at the outset of a TNA to identify all people who are empowered to represent the customer. There may be items in the TNA which require clarification or confirmation as the analysis progresses, and you need to know exactly who to turn to. The consequences of discussing TNA issues with someone who does **not** represent your customer can be quite catastrophic.

Case Study

The Board at J B Plastics asked Ted Fairweather, head of design development, to represent them and commission a TNA to address the problem of falling production standards. Waste was rising, reworking was becoming a major cost, and something had to be done. Ted gave the job to Phil Boon, one of his senior trainers.

Phil Boon treated the two production managers as 'customers' and involved them in early discussions about the desired outcomes of the TNA. These managers effectively steered the TNA and by doing so prejudiced the results. This is precisely what the board did not want to happen.

I don't want to dwell on the political aspects of TNAs, but I have seen too many TNAs ruined because the wrong emphasis was given by someone who should have had no say in the way the process was run, to ignore the danger. You should have no problem in designing an appropriate analysis approach if you stick to the golden rule of focusing on the needs of:

- the customers

    and

- the customers' named representatives.

Summary

In Chapter 1 you saw first how to identify customers. Broadly speaking, a customer:

- has ownership of the completed TNA
- pays for the TNA, or has the authority to give it the go-ahead

You then saw how it is important to deal only with customers or with their appointed representatives when planning a TNA. To do otherwise can be catastrophic.

We also mentioned that much of the responsibility for keeping a TNA on track is yours, because you need to line yourself up with the customer's broad aims; but none the less, a good working relationship with your customer and with their representatives is essential.

Assignment:

Find out who has the potential to be your customer for a TNA in your organization. Would they have ownership of it? Would they pay for it? Would you work to them, or to a representative? And who might the representative(s) be?

Write all the answers to these questions on a sheet of paper. This sheet of paper will be the first in a dossier which you'll build up as you go through this book. The dossier, when complete, will be your guide to a successful TNA.

Clarify the Expectations

I said at the beginning — and keep stressing — that a TNA is a response to a perceived problem and, as such, there must be a desired outcome. So, when the 'phone rings and a key figure requests a TNA, there has to be a point very soon afterwards where you will ask what your customer actually expects.

By the time you've finished this chapter, you will be able to:

- list key questions which you must ask if you're to carry out a successful TNA

- defend your asking of these questions

- respond appropriately if the answers to your questions are not satisfactory.

We'll start by imagining a situation where your customer commissions a TNA without being really sure **why** it's necessary. We've been in this sort of situation:

Trainer: OK, about this TNA. What are you seeking to achieve?

Client: I don't know. I thought you'd be finding out all about that sort of thing . . . .

What do you do in this situation? Think of your own practical course of action and write it in this box.

There is only one thing to do. You must help your customer to clarify their expectations. This should involve:

- explaining your view of a TNA, that is that TNAs are a response to a problem

- explaining that a TNA's only justification is that it will help the business to meet its goals, aim and mission

Then you **ask**:

- what is the problem, and how will it help the organization to have the problem solved?

By taking this position early on in the TNA it will become clear to your customer that the TNA is not something which you can go away and concoct in an ivory tower somewhere. It can only be carried out effectively as a partnership. Your part of the bargain is that you will find out information and present it in a useful and usable format. The customer's part is that he or she will tell you exactly what it is which needs to be achieved.

Some customers are familiar with successful TNAs and will have worked out in some detail what they expect the analysis can achieve for them. Their expectations are likely to be realistic and achievable. Others will need help. Their expectations could be unfocused and unrealistic. In either case we advise you to meet with the customer and ask a series of questions about what the TNA is expected to achieve. The difference between the informed and the uninformed customer is that one will be able to answer your questions easily and in terms you understand and the other won't.

So what should you ask? Before we move on to this it is important, especially when dealing with a customer with unclear expectations, that you are as well informed as possible about your organization. There are some key pieces of information you could usefully have on file. It is all probably in your head but it is also useful when designing a TNA to have it written down. That way it is relatively easy to confirm.

So fill in this form with details of yourself and your situation.

Assignment:

1. *Does your organization have a mission statement? If so, what is it?*

2. *How many people work for your organization in total?*

3. *How many divisions/departments/levels/parts are there?*

4. *How many people do you have in your training team?*

5. *What is morale like in your organization? — and why is this so?*

6. *What do people talk about when they're at work but not 'on duty'?*

Let's get back to the questions you should ask to make sure that your customer's expectations are clear and precise.

Over the years my team has identified 12 questions which it is essential to ask at this stage of a training needs analysis. But, before we describe them, take a minute or two to imagine that when you get to work tomorrow morning you are asked to carry out a TNA. What would be the six main questions you'd ask your customer straight away?

Make a list of the six questions (or more if you really want to) here.

- .

- .

- .

- .

- .

- .

The 12 Questions Essential to the TNA

1. What is the Perceived Problem?

Notice the use of the word 'perceived'. At this stage this is all it is. The real problem may be shown by your analysis to be different to this, but for now the perceived problem is the only one you have to work with. The problem which generates the need must ultimately arise from the mission and aims of the organization. If the problem cannot be linked to these then you should confirm that the TNA really is necessary. But assuming that they are linked you should demonstrate the links formally and in writing.

For example:

1. Suppose the problem is given to you that waste is running at 12 per cent. You know from the organization's aims statement that the target is to reach 3 per cent within 18 months. So the problem is clear: people need to work in a way which reduces waste.

2. Suppose your customer indicates that the problem is that not enough new customers are being attracted by the sales staff. You read the organization's aims and it says that there is a need to increase the number of new customers. So again the problem is clear: people (in this case sales staff) need to work in a way which attracts more customers.

In all cases you should check that your customer's problem or problems match the organization's mission and aims. If they don't, now is the time to make sure that you are not about to embark on an unjustifiable series of actions.

2. What are Your Customer's Aims and Objectives?

This is really two questions but as aims and objectives are in reality usually so closely linked and so often described together, from a practical point of view they are usefully dealt with together. As I noted above, the problem which generates the need for a TNA should be closely linked to both the mission and aims of the organization. And the same is true for the aims and objectives. Take the examples from above.

Example 1 was:

> That waste is running at 12 per cent. You know from the organization's aims statement that the target is to reach 3 per cent within 18 months. This gives you both the problem and the aim for your TNA, which is therefore:
>
> *To identify the developments needed to reduce waste to 3 per cent within the date set in the aims statement.*

Example 2 was:

> That not enough new customers are being attracted by the sales staff. The organization's aims say that we need to increase the number of new customers. However, this is not enough for you. You need a clearer aim for your TNA so that you can clearly target your ultimate recommendations. So between you and your customer you decide that the aim should be:
>
> To identify the developments needed to gain five new customers per year for five years.
>
> Once again, and in all cases, you should check that your customer's aims match with and will help attain the organization's aims and, if not, to make sure that you are not about to embark on an unjustifiable series of actions.
>
> The objectives should add detail to the aims to be achieved. They are the key performance indicators your customer will use to evaluate the outcomes you achieve. These performance indicators should be elicited very carefully as they will guide every step you take though the TNA process. They are likely to be few in number—three or four are typical but you may have more.
>
> You can find out exactly what these indicators are by asking your customer what they would like to use the outcomes of the TNA for. This part of the questioning process should produce a set of actions.

Some examples of customer objectives we have come across include using the outcomes of the training needs analysis to:

- outline a series of costed alternative recommendations
- produce a report which can be circulated among budget holders and will engage their commitment
- develop recommendations which will achieve the aim and cut the resources currently being spent by 50 per cent
- introduce a personal development programme
- increase the efficiency of a department
- demonstrate a commitment to improving the organization's performance
- provide their staff with job-focused training support
- enable a group of staff to operate in teams and receive delegated decision-making powers.

Take a few minutes now to list the questions you would ask of your customer to find out the perceived problem, their aims and their objectives. Keep this list as a future resource. As this list may be quite lengthy, we suggest you use a separate piece of paper.

3. What is the Customer Expecting From the TNA?

It is likely that the TNA will be expected to address a mismatch between actual performance and desired performance, or perhaps, to take a longer view, a mismatch between anticipated performance (given current trends) and desired future performance. However, it is unlikely that the customer will want the mismatch merely confirmed; he or she will want workable solutions.

So a key role for the TNA will be for the training function to suggest strategies, tactics, methods and techniques to address training needs uncovered. This is the key.

It is unreasonable to expect the training function to analyse in depth any other issues which may emerge. However, other issues which are unrelated to the aims of the TNA are more than likely to arise. You should agree with your customer at this point how these issues will be handled. I suggest that you agree to list them as 'Issues to be Addressed Outside the TNA', and if necessary discuss them at a later stage.

Case Study

A major retailer was experiencing serious problems with its customer care. Quite simply the customers weren't always satisfied with the way they were treated, especially if they had a problem such as faulty goods, exchanges or refunds.

A TNA was commissioned which revealed training needs in the areas of interpersonal skills, knowledge of consumer legislation and customer care. A suitable programme of role-playing, workshops, open learning and CBT (computer-based training) was set up so that the groups that needed the skills most received the training first. In other words, the training aspect was identified, addressed and ultimately resolved.

The TNA also revealed flaws in the incentive system: staff dealing with refunds were losing out on possible commission, while their colleagues making new sales weren't. The TNA flagged this as an issue and even went as far as suggesting who should be involved in reviewing the incentive system — but no further. Trainers are not expected to be experts on incentives.

4. Which Group am I Expected to Work With or Have Access to?

It is especially clear in large organizations that not everyone can be involved in the same TNA at the same time. For one thing, the resources of the training function would be overstretched, and for another, the result of the TNA would be something gigantic and unmanageable. When you ask questions in this area, you should press for answers which clearly identify specific groups of people. Answers like the following are fine:

- all clerical staff on the Abingdon site
- all paint-shop employees
- sales staff not based in Bristol.

But if you got an answer like:

- everybody connected with sorting and despatching

— what would you do?

Outline a strategy you would adopt if your customer failed to define accurately the group or groups of people to be involved in the TNA.

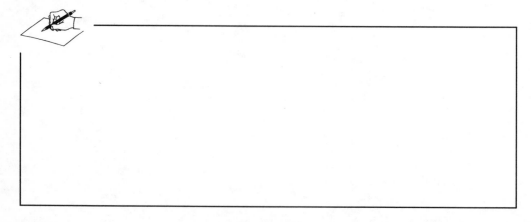

- First, what you **don't** do. You don't accept the vague definition and assume it will become clear when the TNA gets underway. This leads either to a TNA which grows unstoppably, or to one which misses out a group of key employees.

- What you **do** is get the customer to clarify in detail exactly who will be involved and who won't. This list should then be agreed to and signed off.

5. What Performance is Required From the Target Group?

As discussed earlier, the problem should be a mismatch between actual and desired performance within the target group. The challenge from your point of view is to get a definition of desired performance which is:

- achievable

- measurable

- unambiguous.

Many customers are used to working in such areas and will be able to provide very clear definitions of the problem.

Case Study

Part of a government agency approached its training division to carry out a TNA with a view to reducing error rates in over-payments from 5 per cent to 2 per cent in steps of 1 per cent over the next 18 months; the savings needed in administrative costs and in over-payments were all quantified.

The training division was able to produce a report whose recommendations were sharply focused on these figures. The figures also provided the basis for a system to monitor the effectiveness of the proposed training programme.

Be careful not to rule out any problems as unsuited to a TNA before you have considered them very seriously.

The following activity lists one problem and a number of possible causes. After each cause there are three boxes where you can tick **yes**, **no** or **maybe** to state whether or not there is a training response.

Tick one of the three boxes for each possible cause.

Problem: Market Share Falling

	Training Input Relevant?		
Possible causes:	Yes	No	Maybe
1. Increased competitor activity	☐	☐	☐
2. Salespeople can't sell	☐	☐	☐
3. Prices too high	☐	☐	☐
4. Poor product quality	☐	☐	☐

We conclude that the answer has to be at least 'maybe' in every case.

1. Maybe the response to increased competitor activity could be an increase in your own activity, which may require training for certain groups of people.

2. Maybe salespeople who can't sell could be running into problems beyond their control — a recession, a trade embargo or the like. But it could be that they haven't sufficient product knowledge or that they're not working closely enough with their production teams — and those are areas where training is called for.

3. Maybe high prices are due to increases in raw material costs. But they could be due to mistakes and inefficiencies whose costs are being passed on to customers. In the mistakes case, training will be able to improve the situation. Even with the case of high raw material costs, training could point the way to efficencies which could reduce the effect of those high costs.

4.   Maybe poor product quality could be traceable to any number of causes, but human error or indeed human apathy are likely causes. Training can address the problem directly — by improving skills — and indirectly, by making people feel valued and increasing their motivation to do a good job. A good TNA would show whether the answer should be a definite YES.

6. Timescale, or 'How Long Have I Got'?

In many cases there will be a board meeting or other high-powered event at which your report will be presented, so you will certainly need to know when this is to take place. On other occasions, trainers are quizzed:

•   I don't know. How long **d'you** think it will take?

If this is the attitude, the best course of action is to go away and plan out your proposals carefully. You need to bear in mind the other parameters you have to work within — usually:

•   budget
•   staff availability
•   method of data gathering
•   urgency of the problem.

Then you can present and justify your estimate of timescales with all the relevant facts at your disposal. **Don't** commit yourself to a deadline you can't make.

7. How Much Can I Spend?

No customer is going to say 'spend what you like', and most will either allocate you a budget over and above your normal purse or say what proportion of your current budget should be diverted to the TNA. **But there's a third possibility: what is it? Write it in this box.**

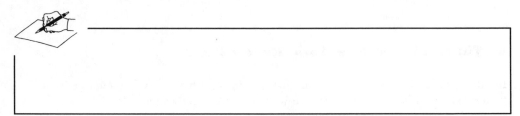

- Your customer may ask you to cost out some options.

If so, this costing task is best carried out as soon as possible after your meeting with the customer. Don't be tempted to produce 'ball-park figures' unless you're pressed. The costing process should cover the same four issues listed under question 6.

8. What Kind of Hindrance Can I Expect?

We said earlier that we don't want to get bogged down in the political machinations of TNAs. But it's a fact of life that if there is a perceived mismatch between actual and desired performance, then someone somewhere will be feeling responsible.

In organizations where there is a pronounced 'blame-culture' — that is to say, where problems are countered not by 'what can we do about that?' but by 'who can we hold responsible?' — then you may meet a good deal of defensiveness when you start asking questions. Even in open organizations, it is in certain individuals' nature to be guarded in their response to questions about performance and perceived performance.

The more information you gather about the potential for your activities to be seen as threatening, the more opportunity you have to design a sympathetic approach to your TNA, one that will allay possible fears and suspicions. Your customer may be able to give you names of individuals and groups who are feeling vulnerable and, of course, you will deal with this with the utmost discretion.

9. How Would Your Customer Like the Information Presented?

This question can be taken either practically or politically.

Practical Considerations

If your customer needs a detailed report for ten people, a summary for 250 affected employees and a presentation with overhead projector transparencies for the board at head office in Delaware, then there are logistical and administrative elements to be borne in mind from the outset, for example:

- Who is going to do the presentation? Yourself? A team?
- How long will the presentation last? An hour? More?
- Who is going to reproduce the report? In what form? Glossy magazine, perhaps, or more practical spiral-bound notepaper?

The production of the report needs to be managed as a separate project with a specific end-date driving all the stages that go before it. You may well find that the end-date for your TNA is a good deal earlier than the end-date for the production of the report.

Political Considerations

When presenting your report you are, in effect, arguing a case for your recommendations. The sooner you can get information about the degree of resistance or compliance you're going to encounter, the better. It will enable you to construct your report in such a way that it has maximum effect.

10. Is Anywhere or Anything Out of Bounds?

The answer you are looking for is 'no'. If you can go anywhere and ask anything, then you can construct your TNA with confidence. But the following case study will demonstrate the dangers of failing to ask about where you can and can't go.

Case Study

A trainer was commissioned to do a TNA to examine what would be necessary to effect a change from hierarchical, function-orientated working to process-orientated team-working. The trainer opted for a questionnaire-based approach, but found that 30 per cent of his chosen respondents weren't able to help. These employees were involved in leading-edge work and were in the final stages of preparing for the launch of a new product, information on which was to be divulged only to those who needed to know.

Had the trainer been aware of the restrictions placed on these people, his questionnaire could have been differently targeted, or at least differently phrased. The result was a TNA which was both delayed and inconclusive.

11. Are There Any Key Issues?

Amongst the customer's aims and objectives may be one or two which are paramount. To give these the same treatment as other aims and objectives will be to disappoint the customer.

12. Are There Any Special Questions I Should Ask?

Answers to the 11 areas above are essential to all trainers preparing a TNA. If there are any issues peculiar to your situation which the 11 questions haven't addressed, then you must ask more questions. For example, you could have a prior commitment — say, five or six of your key team members running long courses for the next month or two.

We cannot say what peculiar issues or obstacles may be affecting your ability to deliver what your customer needs, but whatever they may be, they need bringing to light at an early stage.

When you've got your answers to all your questions, what is your essential next step? Write it in here:

- The next step is to get the customer to agree, in writing, to the points which, between you, you have clarified.

In practice this means that you will have to prepare a draft agreement to be signed by yourself and your customer which commits both of you to the TNA as described in the agreement. This may seem an unnecessarily formal thing to do, but there are a number of advantages for both you and your customer in this course of action.

First, you are protected to some extent from that scourge of the professional trainer: the customer who changes his mind.

Second, as you are questioning your customer, one or two issues will crop up which you may need time to reflect on. Your thoughts and suggestions can all be incorporated into the draft agreement for your customer to approve in detail.

Third, your customer has a clear description of the objectives and outcomes they can expect to see and receive.

Finally, you both have a set of agreed points against which to evaluate the outcomes of the whole process.

The document should contain the answers to all the questions which you have had answered, although you may prefer to use different terminology. For example, where you asked 'What is the customer expecting from the TNA?' a paragraph with bullet points, entitled 'Desired Outcomes' would do the trick. Similarly, 'How long have I got?' could become 'Timing' or 'Timescale'. These changes are merely cosmetic. The important point is to get all your goals and parameters down in writing and then to get the customer to sign up to them.

Questions to Ask — A Summary

When you are discussing a TNA with your customer, you need to ask the following questions:

1. What is the perceived problem?
2. What are your aims and objectives?
3. What are you expecting from the TNA?
4. Which group am I expected to work with or have access to?
5. What performance is required from the target group?
6. Timescale, or 'How long have I got'?
7. How much can I spend?
8. What kind of hindrance can I expect?
9. How would you like the information to be presented?
10. Is anywhere or anything out of bounds?
11. Are there any key issues?
12. Are there any special questions I should ask?

When you have answers to those questions, you should compile them into a document which your customer should then sign. This document is the basis of a contract between you and your customer.

Assignment:

Add to the dossier you began at the end of Chapter 1 a template for an agreement between you and your customer covering all the aspects which you need clarified at the beginning of a TNA. Make sure the paragraph headings are all in place and that they cover all the points you would need to clarify.

Take the document to the people who are likely to commission a TNA and explain its purpose to them.

Design the Training Needs Programme

By this stage you are aware that you have a complex task on hand, and only limited resources with which to complete it in a given time. Your programme must primarily meet the customer's needs. This must be your focus rather than the time and resources factors. In other words you should focus:

- first, on what needs to be done
- second, on the most efficient and practicable means of doing it.

By the time you've completed this chapter, you will be able to:

- describe the types of analysis most commonly used
- explain how to list the locations where the data can be found
- explain the features and benefits of successful ways of collecting data
- state the steps you would take to prepare to analyse the data which comes in.

What Needs to be Done

Preparing a training needs analysis programme is a task which can be broken down into three main areas:

- deciding the type of analysis you wish to use

- deciding how to collect the data
- identifying key points to bear in mind as you ask your questions

You need to look at each area in turn.

1. Types of Analysis

Your first decision will concern the type of analysis you intend to employ. We are not talking about mathematical and statistical considerations here, but about the overall focus of your analysis. In our experience there are two possibilities:

- Job analysis

  and
- Outcome analysis

Job Analysis

In a job analysis, what is it that you actually analyse?

A job analysis involves looking at . . .

- A job analysis involves looking at what people **do**.

Of course, there is more to it than that. The job analysis will reveal matches and mismatches, as this case study shows.

Case Study

The incoming mail office at Graxxon Enterprises had a team of four employees who took arriving mail and sorted it for delivery by trolley at 11.15 each morning.

The job analysis revealed that some of what they did was quite efficient. They had evolved, over and above the requirement of their job descriptions, a system of sort-codes and task divisions within the office which made for an efficient dispatch of the mail. This was a close match of job requirement and skills available.

The analysis also revealed awareness of what to do with unnamed, non-specific mail — maybe in the form of mailshots from potential suppliers. Who was 'Head of Standards Development'? What standards? What department? The mailsort team had a list of strategically placed 'friendly faces' in most areas of the business whom they could ring up and ask if it sounded likely that they knew who was the intended recipient. When questioned, the mailsort team did not really know even in the broadest terms what went on in many departments and this was identified as a mismatch, and consequently a training need.

Outcome Analysis

A different slant arises if you use an outcome analysis. Outcome analysis focuses on the outcomes which people are expected to produce. These are the desired outcomes if they are to help the company achieve its mission. From these it is possible to work out what they **should** be doing. We said at the outset that we feel that value-added activities are the key to commercial success and, by analysing outcomes in terms of the mission, you do achieve a value-added focus to your TNA. The application of outcomes analysis is explained in full in Kogan Page's *Functional Analysis* by James Jones. For TNA purposes a functional analysis comprises these questions:

- what do you achieve?

- what do you need to achieve?
- what training would you need to help you achieve your desired outcome?

It may be that an outcomes analysis will result in the same recommendations as a job analysis, but this is not guaranteed, because in many organizations what people do is not the same as what they should be doing; and what they feel they need to do is not the same as what they really need to do.

2. Data Collection

Data means, literally, things which are given. In a TNA, one set of facts is given at a very early stage: the desired outcome as described and agreed by yourself and your customer. This leaves one set of data to be collected: the data which describe the current state of affairs, from which you will be able to analyse what the needs are. The data you'll need divide into two sorts:

- hard data
- soft data.

Hard Data

Hard data are facts you can find out from:

- reading things
- checking documents
- combing through reports
- business records
- administrative reports.

It's all to do with incontrovertible facts, 'there in black and white'.

Soft Data

Soft data, on the other hand, are details of:

- what people think
- what people hope for and fear
- how people perceive things.

Of the two types of data, which do you think is most important for a TNA, and why?

Many trainers, when asked to prioritize hard and soft data, pick **hard**: but consider the following illustration.

Case Study

Production workers at Barker Smith and Newton took part in a TNA the aims of which were to increase production by 10 per cent over the next year and a half.

The production team claimed to be disenchanted with management because they were being 'kept in the dark'. Consequently, when it came to making extra efforts, sacrifices of time, or considering new ways of tackling jobs, the staff were less than whole-heartedly enthusiastic. Views such as these were to be found everywhere:

- they never tell us what to do or enough in advance!
- nobody tells anybody anything round here!

The hard facts however, contradicted these perceptions: there was a fortnightly bulletin handed to every employee which explained what targets had been met, reports on recent management team meetings and appeals for people's ideas.

The problem was that all the bulletins in the world couldn't alter the workers' perception of the state of affairs. Had the TNA concentrated on hard facts alone, then in-company communications would have got a clean bill of health, and no recommendations would have been made in that area.

So it is the **soft** data which are more important. The reason for this is that it is people's perceptions which guide their behaviour, rather than hard facts. The hard facts may form the basis for desired behaviour, but without knowing people's current perceptions the actions needed to effect the required change cannot be designed. In this case study the TNA took great account of the perceptions, so one recommendation was that senior managers carry out a training programme to enable them to:

- communicate with their staff effectively.

The Data List

It is likely that for every area or group of people you're expected to work with there will be soft data **and** hard data.

Listing Your Data

Before you do anything else in your TNA, you need to list the data — or potential sources of data — in a **structured** way. There are many types of structure which could be used, but they will vary in their effectiveness. An alphabetical list, for example, may be difficult to compile and difficult to use when you actually get round to gathering the data at a later stage.

How would you structure your data collection? List the headings you would use here.

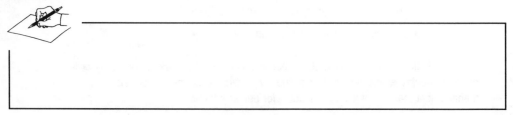

It's not possible to comment on your list in detail but you might find it useful to compare it with my data list structure.

I have always found it easier and much more effective to structure a data list according to target group, type of data and location — as in this example:

Target group	Soft data	Hard data	Location/Access
Head Office staff	Perceptions about —performance —feedback —training received —value	Minutes Memos Performance measures	Files Files Personnel office

After each item in the list, it is worth writing down:

- **where** the information may be obtained
  and
- **who** can provide information, and **when**.

Designing a Way to Gather Soft Data

Given that soft data come from people's thoughts and perceptions, what methods would you suggest for gathering them?

Write two possibilities in this box.

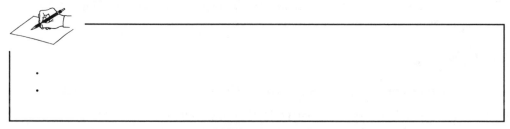

-
-

There are basically two effective methods: interviews and questionnaires.

You'll notice we say interviews **and** questionnaires because there is no reason why one should be used to the exclusion of the other. In fact, the soundest of TNAs employ both questionnaires and interviews, with the views expressed in both corroborating each other. There are three things to consider:

- first, in which circumstances are interviews to be preferred over questionnaires, and vice versa?

- second, when and how can interviews and questionnaires be combined?

- third, how do you design interviews and questionnaires?

Interviews Preferred

Interviews are to be preferred when there are relatively small numbers of people involved. The definition of 'relatively small' will of course vary from organization to organization, so, for practical purposes, if you and your team have time to interview all the people whose views you need — and to analyse the results — then use the interview approach. The benefits are as follows:

- you will be able to react to fine nuances of meaning

- you can encourage the respondent to co-operate more easily

- assuming no cancellations — you are assured of a very high rate of returns; 100 per cent is not unusual

- the respondents will remember the interview experience when the results of the TNA become known

- interviews make the respondents feel valued — they've played a personal part in the consultation process

The disadvantages are that interviews:

- are time-consuming for interviewer and respondent

- are prone to greater inconsistency than questionnaires, in that the interviewer cannot guarantee to ask the same question in the same way time after time

Questionnaires Preferred

Questionnaires are preferred when there are large numbers of people whose views you need to consider — too many to interview. They are cheap to reproduce, relatively easy to distribute and, provided they are designed to be easy to fill in, they can be simple to complete and to analyse. The advantages of questionnaires are:

- low cost
- high coverage
- ease of analysis
- consistency of message
- permanence of data; there is always a prime record to return to in case of dispute or ambiguity

The disadvantages are that questionnaires:

- need a lot of design work if they are to be effective
- rarely, if ever, yield up 100 per cent returns; 70 per cent — 90 per cent is a good average, 30 per cent — 40 per cent is more normal
- lower return rates involve the analyst in extrapolations— interpreting what the findings **would** mean if applied to the whole workforce

Interviews and Questionnaires Combined

We said earlier that interviews and questionnaires can be used in tandem, and that the best results often involve this two-method approach. One case would be where there are two groups of people for you to interview. The first group comprises, say, 20 people. The second comprises 200. The first group receive an interview, the second a questionnaire. But the effectiveness of the data-gathering could be enhanced by combining interviews and questionnaires in a slightly different way.

In the box below, suggest how you would combine interviews and questionnaires when analysing two groups: one of 20 people and, as part of the same TNA, a group of 200.

- · The first group can be interviewed, and this will yield ample data.
- · A small **sample** of the second group can be interviewed, and the results of their interviews can be used:
  - — as raw data in their own right
  - — to guide the design of a questionnaire for the whole of the second group (including interviewees) to complete.

You will learn more about this on page 54 when we look in some detail at the key issues of questionnaire design.

Designing a Way to Gather Hard Data

The most difficult aspect of gathering hard data is finding the data in the first place. Once you know where they are you can, by and large, pull them onto your desk and process them — but more about that in Chapter 6, which deals with making sense of your findings. Broadly speaking, you can find hard data in:

- · written form
- · electronic form
- · observation of practice and procedure

Gathering Written Data

Your TNA design must incorporate a list of all the written sources of information you may need to have access to.

Think for a moment about the kinds of hard data you might want to refer to as part of a TNA in your organization. List up to four here.

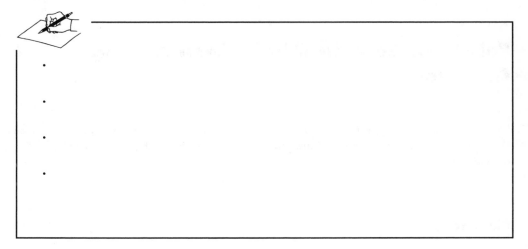

Here is our list. Compare it with yours:

- Company accounts
- Departmental budgets
- Variance analyses
- Results of previous training
- Internal memos
- Company newsletters
- Newspaper items
- Minutes from meetings
- Standards documents.

It is for you to decide at the planning stage whether you are able to extract the data you need from this source material 'on location' or whether it is better to bring everything back to your desk and sift through it there. The criteria to apply is always the amount of material to be gone through. If the amount is small, take it back to your desk.

Points to Bear in Mind When Asking Questions

So far in this chapter you have seen when interviews and questionnaires are appropriate, but you have not considered what needs to be in the questionnaires or interviews.

Simplicity

The by-word when you're compiling interviews and questionnaires is **simplicity**. By keeping it simple, whatever you decide to include will need to be understood unambiguously by the respondents and, at a later stage, by the analysts.

There is nothing more infuriating than discovering that large numbers of your questionnaire respondents appear to be signalling something really unexpected . . . and then to notice that it's probably because they've misinterpreted the question. It's also embarrassing to be conducting a carefully-prepared interview, and to be asked, 'Are you asking me whether I **have** those skills or I **need** this skill? It's not clear,' and then to realize for the first time that, yes, it is unclear what you mean.

You can't always guarantee to achieve 100 per cent consistent comprehensibility; every stick has two ends, and if it's possible to get hold of the wrong end of the stick, someone somewhere will do it. But it will certainly help matters if you use clear, simple language. Clear, simple language is always less ambiguous than complex jargon, so don't worry about appearing inexpert or naive. Just use simple, direct sentences and ordinary words.

Address All the Points

We can't go into the complexities of questionnaire design here. Effective
questionnaire design is an extensive and comprehensive subject in its own right.
Our main goal here is learning about training needs and how to identify and respond
to them. None the less, when you are preparing your questions you must ensure that
all the issues you're supposed to be exploring are actually being explored. The
simplest and most effective way of making sure all of the issues are covered is to
use a check-list. A piece of paper divided into three vertical columns will be
sufficient. Down the left-hand side you write down the points you're exploring. In
the middle column you identify which of the objectives for the TNA the area to be
addressed relates to. The right-hand side remains blank until your first draft
questionnaire or interview is ready. Then you write the numbers of the questions
which relate to each point next to each point. Once you've been through the whole
of your draft, you should check:

- that all areas have been covered

- that no one area has received excessive attention

- that no one area has been neglected.

Below there's an example of the sort of thing we mean. Notice that the 'area to be
addressed' has been broken down into its constituent parts.

Area to be Addressed	Linked to Objective	Questions Asked
1. Training		
a. Perceptions of recent training	—what do people think about training?	Q3, Q4, Q5
b. Perceptions of current training		Q3, Q6, Q7
c. Perceptions of anticipated training		Q3, Q8-12

Flexibility

When you're sure of all the questions you need, then stop and think. Be ready to admit the possibility that you may have:

- approached the situation with some false assumptions
- overlooked something which is obvious to the respondents, in view of their experience and everyday tasks
- inadvertently raised suspicions or doubts in the respondent's mind

How can you accommodate this situation in your questionnaire or interview? Write a suggestion in the box below.

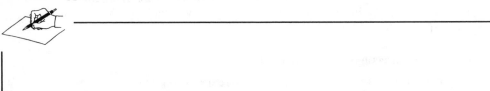

We have found success by adding a final question at the end of an interview along the lines of:

- 'Are there any questions you feel we should have asked?'

This allows the interviewee or the questionnaire respondent to flag up all those areas which might rankle and fester if they are not brought to the surface. The advantages are two or sometimes three-fold.

- Every time, the person providing the data will feel **involved**.
- Every time, you will get the chance to identify wide-held perceptions if there are lots of people all bringing up the same point. One-off perceptions can be obtained, and then you can ignore them if they are clearly just one person's biased view, or alternatively, if the one-off perception has the germ of a genuine clear insight into the problem, you can include it in your findings.
- If these perceptions come to light as part of an interview which precedes a questionnaire, they can then be incorporated into the questionnaire proper.

Ensuring Co-operation

Sometimes you may find yourself interviewing someone who obviously isn't interested. Not that they're obstructive, just that they're not committed to the interview as you'd like. As for questionnaires, you can't guarantee that people will fill them in.

In a short sentence, what is the best way of ensuring that your data providers will co-operate with your TNA? Write it in here.

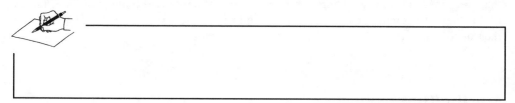

  •   The best way to ensure co-operation is to **sell the benefits**.

In practice, this means including in the script for your interview, or the rubric of your questionnaire, some idea of the potential benefits of your TNA. Many interviewers think that it is sufficient to explain that you're not involved in a hatchet job; that your prime aim is not to seek out the inefficient with a view to making them redundant. We reckon that this tactic will serve chiefly to alarm the people you're talking to, especially if it is used without an explanation of what potential benefits are anticipated. Compare your own experiences at the doctor's or the dentist's. Did you **believe** them when they said it wasn't going to hurt? Or would you have preferred a more honest appraisal of the situation: 'This injection may sting a little bit, after that you won't feel a thing . . . '.

Finally, don't forget to thank the people for their co-operation. It's a small point but it's an important one.

Matching Subsequent Analytical Techniques

Your interview or questionnaire must produce results which are consistent and are capable of being analysed by your chosen technique. To ignore this fundamental point is to court disaster. You could imagine a situation where two analysts go into a department and employ different techniques. One designed his questions so that they could all be answered in terms of a scale from nought to ten. The other asked questions with two possible responses; 'unhappy' and 'delighted'. Comparing results would be a nightmare — so consistency is the key. Similarly you should start off with an analytical technique in mind, so that you can structure your questions and their responses correctly. There are more details of analytical techniques in Chapter 6. For now it is enough to ensure that you don't assume you gather the data first and then decide how to analyse it.

Practicalities

It is almost impossible to overstate the importance of getting a good response to your questioning initiatives. Consequently, there must be clear guidelines to the people filling in your questionnaires as to when and how (or to whom) to return them. Many trainers involved in large TNAs will set up and publicize in advance special means of collection — perhaps temporary letter-boxes or dockets. The advantage of this particular tactic lies in more than its being an effective means of data collection; temporary furniture of any sort acts as a reminder to all who use it that there is a special event taking place.

The Final Steps in Designing the Plan

Following the principles outlined in the second half of this chapter, we believe a successful TNA questionnaire should be composed as follows:

1. Explanation of why this is being done

2. Explanation of the benefits of everyone filling it in
3. The questions
4. Instructions for returning the completed form
5. Thanks for co-operation.

Once you have designed your TNA programme, what do you think is the very next step? Write your answer in this box.

Once the TNA programme is designed, the next step is to . . .

- The next step is to submit your detailed plan to the customer for approval.

There are two main reasons why this approval is essential. First, it endows your data-collection with the ultimate authority, and you cannot be accused of interfering where you have no business, or meddling in areas you don't understand. We alluded earlier to one TNA which had come unstuck because many of the people questioned were involved in secret work. Your customer's approval can overcome any such barriers. Alternatively — and here we move on to the second advantage — if your plan inadvertently trespasses into an area of genuine sensitivity then your customer can withhold approval until you redesign your programme. This means there is no chance of your committing yourself to a course of action which you cannot complete.

Summary

This long and fairly detailed chapter showed you first of all:

- the two types of analysis most commonly used, namely, job analysis and outcome analysis.

You then moved on to see:

- the importance of listing all the data you will need to complete your TNA.

We stressed the existence of hard data and soft, and showed why soft data are often more relevant than hard, because they relate to people's perceptions.

The chapter then moved on to the importance of gathering your data in such a way that they can lead to accurate, meaningful and practicable recommendations, which in turn means that in your planning stage you have to be clear, unambiguous, friendly, open, and honest so as to obtain maximum co-operation from your people.

Finally you saw the importance of getting your prepared plan signed off by your customer.

Assignment:

1. *Prepare a **data list** to support the work you're planning to do in your TNA. Remember to include soft and hard data and their location.*

2. *Plan out a script for an interview or a questionnaire, ensuring it has the five principles contained in this chapter embedded in it. Include this questionnaire/interview in your TNA plan when you submit it to your customer.*

3. *Draw up a complete TNA plan to submit to your customer. Ensure the customer realizes there is an opportunity to negotiate the content or the stucture of the TNA at this point.*

Arrange Access to Data

Following hard on the heels of a long chapter about planning your TNA, Chapter 4 will seem short. Short does not mean trivial or unimportant, however, and this step — arranging access — is actually imperative if your TNA is to succeed. By the time you've finished this chapter you will be able to:

- list, in sequence, the steps you should take to ensure you will be able to get hold of the data you need for your TNA.

First, we'd like to show you the consequences of **not** arranging access to data.

Case Study

J K Lenses undertook a TNA in response to a perceived threat from Japanese competition. They went for an outcome analysis which required in its early stages access to the detailed business objectives of the organization. They planned to gather these hard data in April, and arranged a series of interviews with senior managers for May. One of the semi-autonomous divisions of J K Lenses was revising its business plan during the month of April in view of greater than expected successes, and so consequently had no current data to hand over. The interviews in May had to be postponed and the whole TNA lost credibility.

A Plan of Campaign

You already know, as part of your data list what data you need and where those data can be located.

The next stage is to identify in respect of every item of data the name of a person who can provide access to the data or who has the authority to permit you access to it. Normally, this will involve a quick phone call, during which you will clarify:

- what data you need
- when you need them by
- why you need them
- whether the person you've called can provide the help you need, or if not the name of someone who can.

To omit any of these points will cause, at best, confusion. At worst, you'll get a refusal. The person you contact will say, 'I'm sorry, I'll have to check with so-and-so that we can give you what you need. Can I call you next week?' You see what's happened. You have lost a week off your schedule before you have even started, and if you try to cut corners to redeem the situation, you risk antagonizing lots of people.

If it is hard data you are seeking, a secretary, librarian or archivist may be able to grant access — but put yourself in their position. The librarian may be willing to help, but if the trawl for your data is going to tie up library staff and/or library equipment for long periods at busy times, then with the best will in the world, you may face a refusal.

If you are seeking soft data, then a similar sequence of events must take place. You must inform not only the interviewees but their managers or the rest of their team:

- who you need to interview
- what it is about
- what the purpose of the interview will be
- when you need to have the interviews completed.

Just as with hard data, there may be a valid reason, usually connected with workloads or deadlines, why the managers may say no. The consequences of a refusal for you need not be dire if they are incorporated at the planning stage. The real disasters occur when you assume that everyone will be both willing and able to comply with your requests all the time and, frankly, that is not always the case.

Put your practical hat on for a minute, and say what you would do in this situation: You have three months from initial brief to final recommendation to complete your TNA. You have decided to interview each of the 12 laboratory scientists. However, your request to interview is refused. They are too busy on a six-month project to spare the two hours each you have requested for the interviews.

Write in here what you would do.

Well there are a number of possibilities here:

1. **You could change the interview to a questionnaire —** questionnaires can be filled in as and when the respondents have time, and you can make a virtue of reacting to their concerns about the limited time available.

2. **You could identify a small number of key questions and request very short interviews —** say 10 to 15 minutes each. Prioritizing the parts of the data list to be addressed in the shorter interviews may mean prejudging the issues. However, you could use a shorter interview followed by a questionnaire.

3. **You could retain the need for two-hour interviews and renegotiate the deadline with your customer —** in all probability you would have to have a very good justification for this course of action to be acceptable.

4. **You could select a small sample from the group and only interview them —** this might give you the highest level of accuracy but doesn't avoid the problem they all perceive they have, that of not enough time to justify taking two hours out for an interview.

On balance, option 2 is probably the best if the questionnaire is included, but the most likely option to receive the go-ahead is option 1. You may have thought of others which would be suitable in your organization. If the worst case occurs and you are refused any sort of access to the intended target group you will have to take advice from your customer.

Access Plan

You are now in a position to develop your data collection list into an access plan, which will allow you to note down not only what you need and where it is, but also:

·   who you should contact and

·   what their reaction was.

When all your data is accessible, the collection can begin. Here is our example of a data access plan.

Target group	Type of data soft/hard	Location	Access		
			Who approves?	Approval requested (date)	Approval given (date)

Summary

This short chapter has dealt with:

- why it is essential to arrange access to data
- the people who can grant or refuse access to data
- reasons why people may refuse
- strategies to adopt if access is refused.

You also now have a tool which will enable you to ensure that you can access all data before you commit yourself irrevocably to a course of action which you may not be able to complete on time.

Assignment:
Draw up a data access plan for your TNA.

Collect the Data

In view of all the preparation you have done, this chapter is potentially the shortest in the book. It's expressible in two words:

·   Do it!

Although it can be expressed in two words, this part of the TNA is the most critical. Without this stage you have no TNA. The data are the key. By the time you have finished this chapter, you will be able to:

·   explain and defend at least one practical system for data gathering and monitoring

·   describe common pitfalls and distractions in the field of data gathering and how to avoid them.

Collect as a Project

A TNA is invariably a project which you will undertake as part of your duties as a trainer. But within that project, data collection exists as a mini-project in its own right.

What are the key elements you should include in managing and monitoring data collection? List them in this box.

Your data collection project should have the following features:

- objectives
- correct sequence
- start date
- end date
- resources.

These combine into the acronym OCSER which may help you to remember the headings.

Objectives

In your data collection there will be certain things which have to be done and, when they are done, you will be able to demonstrate they have been completed. We would say that 'talk to all the people concerned' is not really an objective. True, it has to be done, but how could you actually prove you have talked to **all** the people? Objectives are best when they are tightly defined and specific, for example:

- explain the reasons for the TNA to the 12 members of the laboratory team.

Correct Sequence

The objectives have to be met in a workable order. For example, 'Interview the laboratory team' must follow 'Prepare the interview questions' and not precede it. In some cases, the sequence of data collection may be strictly linear, that is to say, each of the steps can only be started when the previous step is completed, thus:

Week 1	Prepare interview questions
Week 2	Print interview script proforma
Week 3	Interview laboratory staff
Week 4	Send completed proformas to office for analysis

In other circumstances, two activities may be able to run concurrently, if, for example, you are interviewing one small group and giving questionnaires to a larger group. The example below shows the sort of thing we mean. Notice that where you run two strands of a project in parallel, there are still places where the strands must meet.

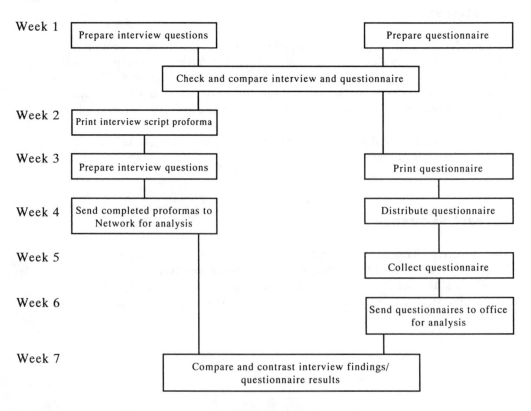

In cases where the results of the interviews are themselves used to create questionnaires, then, clearly, the sequencing will be different. The sequencing also depends on the resources you have available — and we will cover that on the next page under 'Resources'.

Start Date

You should commit yourself at an early stage to a start date for each stage of your data collections, and you should ensure that everyone who is involved in the running of the project knows what those dates are, and agrees to them.

End Date

Similarly each stage should have an end date. The end date will be determined by . . . well, we'll pass that question over to you.

What factors influence the end date of each stage of the data collection project? List them here.

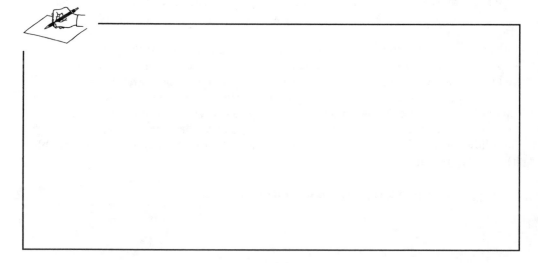

The end date is invariably determined by:

- the size of the task
- the requirements of the overall TNA timescale, which depend on the customer's needs
- the resources you have available.

We would counsel you to leave, where possible, contingency time between the end of one stage and the start of the next. In our experience, data collection often takes longer than anticipated. On the whole, however, the advantages of imposing a disciplined end date far outweigh the problems which can be caused by a 'let's wait and see how long the information takes to come in' approach. But remember to anticipate a little overrun.

Resources

The resources you have at your disposal will determine exactly how you approach your data collection. Solo trainers may be obliged to adopt a linear approach, with one strand of events following after the other. Trainers with teams may be able to divide up the collection into several concurrent strands. It is up to you to decide which option will make the most sense in your circumstances. However, if you choose to involve a team make sure they all know what everyone else is doing.

The resources available will affect the end date of each stage of the project. Experience will tell you how much data one person can collect in one day, but if you're contemplating your first TNA, we advise you not to overstretch yourself. Interviews are time-consuming to prepare properly; questionnaires which can be analysed quickly take a long time to prepare; and carrying out interviews is a draining experience for the interviewer. By the end of the fifth hour spent interviewing, concentration starts to wander, and the results may become unreliable. The golden rule is:

- **allow enough time for data collection.**

Other aspects of a TNA can be compressed, in that overtime may be a possibility for your analysts or yourself. But the data collection won't be hurried.

Pitfalls

Trainers must beware of pitfalls when gathering data, and the prime one is **distraction**. We stressed earlier that you should give everyone you question the opportunity to make their own statement in addition to your prepared questions. The problem arises when the people make surprising and interesting statements. Trainers may make the assumption that whatever they are told must have some bearing on the TNA, and that everybody's suggestion or grievance must be included in the fabric of the final report. As a rule of thumb, to be included in the fabric of the final report, 'stray' comments must be:

- widely held, and/or
- of obvious relevance to the desired outcome of the TNA.

Isolated or less relevant comments can be included, for the sake of completeness, in a 'miscellaneous comments' appendix.

Other pitfalls occur when the principles outlined earlier in this chapter are ignored. For example, some TNAs founder if the data are gathered before the trainer has completed adequate preparation: people simply go and see what they can find out before they really know what they are looking for. Alternatively, the analysis can be started before some of the key data are available, and this may lead to problems.

Summary

Chapter 5 has shown you the importance of organizing your data collection so as to take account of the need for:

- **Objectives** — the tasks which need to be done, described in a specific and measurable way.

- **Correct sequencing** — ensuring that the stages in your data collection which need to follow each other actually do follow each other.

- **Start dates** — which commit you to beginning the collection stages on time.

- **End dates** — so that every stage has a deadline by which time it must be completed. End dates are worked out according to customer needs, the resources you have available and the size of the task.

- **Resources** — only you know the staff and the technology at your disposal, but you should not overstretch yourself.

The chapter then stressed the need to allow enough time for data collection because it is a non-compressible part of the TNA. It concluded with a view of how to cope with three common pitfalls: distraction, faulty sequencing and premature analysis.

Assignment:

1. *If you're using this book to help you through a TNA, use a grid like the one below to plan out your sequencing of events.*

Task \ Week No.	1	2	3	4	5	6	7	8
Design interviews								
Design questionnaires								
Compare questions								
Interview								
Distribute questionnaire								
Collect questionnaires								
etc								
etc								

2. *Prepare and use a parallel grid like the one below to map out resource requirements*

Task \ Week No.	1	2	3	4	5	6	7	8
Who required								
What required								

Keep a record of the occasion when you book someone's services, and confirm your booking in writing.

Make Sense of the Findings

This chapter will focus on making sense of the data you have collected, and by the time you've reached the end of it, you'll be able to:

- analyse data in a simple but meaningful way
- group the data so that they relate exactly to the customer's needs.

These objectives are, after all, the keys to a successful interpretation of all the data you've gathered. Remember, by the time you reach this stage you are likely to have much more information than you need or expected to have. In either case you need to start pruning the information down to the point where you have only the information to . . . to what?

What do you want to achieve with this stage in the process? Write your ideas here.

There are two main things you need to achieve at this stage:

- identify the patterns in the data
- sort out what the patterns mean.

At the end of this part of the process you want to be in a position to prepare a set of recommendations for your customer, to enable them to meet their objectives.
You should also be in a position to support your recommendations with a clear presentation of the results.

Analysing the data

Patterns

The first step in this part of the process is to identify the patterns in the data you have collected, so that you can use them to say something about the population you collected the data from. You have to be able to make comments with enough confidence to recommend one or more courses of action as a result of your findings. So you will have to analyse the data in a way which brings out the patterns.

But remember, you are not the only one who will be using the product of your analysis. Your customer will also be using them. So you need to make sure they can understand, make sense of and use your product as easily as possible. The key watchwords here are to keep whatever you produce **clear** and **simple**.

To do this you need to be clear yourself about exactly what the patterns are and what they show. However, you're likely to have a great deal of data, some in numbers, some in written or verbal form, some soft and some hard data. So to make the analysis easy to understand you should aim to reach a level of uniformity in the way you handle the data.

But first, what do you have to do to identify the patterns in the data? Write a short sentence here to describe what you would do.

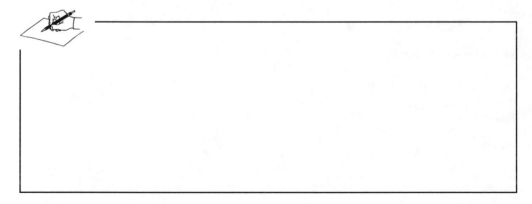

To identify the patterns and trends and make them stand out, you'll have to analyse the data in one of a variety of ways. Then once they are analysed you'll have to group them to enable you to draw conclusions and identify the main comments to be made about each part of the data collected.

Statistics

It's about here in our TNA courses that somebody usually mentions the dreaded word 'statistics', at which point eyes glaze over and people prepare to go home. Statistical analysis does have a key part to play in training needs analyses, but I'd like to make one thing clear now. With the right kind of design there's no reason why you should have to be involved in statistical work which uses any algebra more complex than you'd learned by the time you were 13. It will be a great help to you if you can convert all of your raw findings into numbers so that you can identify trends and patterns more easily. Some questions are likely to have been answered in numbers or may have involved selecting 'yes' or 'no' so these responses can be counted. Other questions might have included written comments. With written comments it is helpful to categorize the comments made under a number of key headings. Once that's done you can then count the number of times a particular comment appears, then average and graph the results. Remember that you want your report to be clear and simple. So use clear and simple statistics.

The most likely statistical techniques you will use for analysing TNA data are:

- mean scores and range

with a lesser likelihood of:

- standard deviation
- correlations
- significance and
- calculation of error being involved.

In this short book there is not the scope to enter into a long section on statistics and how and when they should be used. There is a whole range of books available from Kogan Page which deal with statistical analysis of data and I recommend that you look at a few of them if you need help. For now let's look at an example from a TNA questionnaire:

Example 1

	None at all				All I need
1. How much training have you had for the job you do now?	1	2	3	4	5

How would you analyse the results of the above question?

There are at least two possibilities:

1. *You could count the numbers of respondents choosing each category* and report the totals. It's certainly a simple approach and the outcome will be clear. However, such an approach is too simple. Before you could identify the implications of such a result you really need to know what proportion of the population chose each category.

So the pattern would be much clearer if, after counting the number of responses in each category, you then went on to:

2. *Calculate the percentages of people selecting each category.* This gives you further information about the pattern.

You could draw conclusions at this point but your information base would be further enhanced by knowing the range of selections made.

3. *Identify the range of selections.* If all five categories are used you would draw different conclusions than you would if only 1, 2 and 3 were used **or** if only 4 and 5 were used.

Try working through the example here.

Suppose the total selections for each category were as below; complete the table by filling in the % column:

Category	Total times selected	% Selecting each
1	15	
2	70	
3	90	
4	10	
5	15	

The percentages from 1 to 5 should be:

7.5

35

45

5

7.5

The range is 1 to 5.

So what does this result tell you? Write your ideas in the box below.

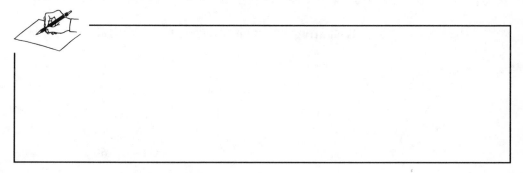

In this case only 12.5 per cent of the people questioned thought that they had had all, or close to all, they needed in the way of training for their current job. However, almost half (45 per cent) were sufficiently happy to have selected the middle of the road score of 3. So is the result positive or negative?

Well, to some extent it depends on the standard the organization considers to be acceptable, but there is a way of using the raw scores to show a negative or positive result.

Take the same Example 1:

Category	Total times selected
1	15
2	70
3	90
4	10
5	15

But this time give each category a weighting. The positive categories get a positive weighting, the negative categories receive a negative weighting and the middle gets a zero weighting. Then write in the number of times selected and calculate the score for each category as follows:

Category	Weighting	Times selected	Score
1	-2	15	-30
2	-1	70	-70
3	0	90	0
4	+1	10	10
5	+2	15	30
			TOTAL -60

Then divide the total by the total number of respondents (200) and you're left with a negative score: **-0.3.** With this kind of weighted scoring analysis a mean score of 1.00 or more indicates a high consensus of a positive nature, 0 means little consensus and -1.0 or a higher negative number means that there is a high consensus of a negative nature. You might like to have a try yourself at this next example using both percentages and weighted scoring analyses: note that there is also a restricted range in this example.

Example 2

2. How would you rate the quality of the training you have had for the job you do now?	Very Good	Quite Good	Neither Good nor Poor	Quite Poor	Very Poor
	1	2	3	4	5
(Times selected)	(0)	(80)	(30)	(30)	(0)

Our analysis is on page 78. The advantage of both the percentage and weighted methods of analysis is that the results can be presented graphically. Graphs and/or tables should be used wherever possible to demonstrate results, as they help both you and your readers to see the patterns clearly.

Taking Example 1 the graphs would look like this:

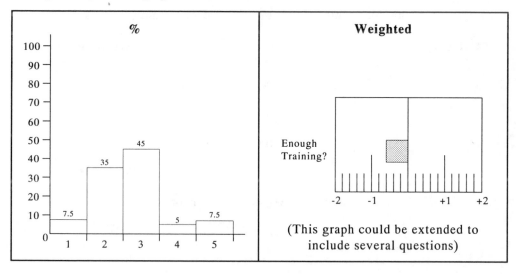

(This graph could be extended to include several questions)

Once you have completed the analysis of each question you can begin to sort out what the analysis means. This process is further helped by grouping the data.

Grouping the Data

In Chapter 2 you looked at clarifying your customer's expectations. Part of the process was to find out what your customer's aims and objectives were for the TNA and then to have your customer agree to them. In Chapter 3 on page 51, you saw the importance of linking the objectives to the areas to be addressed and then with the questions asked. In this part of making sense of the data you should return to that table on page 51 and collect together the analyses for all of the questions in a particular groups, eg group 1a, questions 3, 4 and 5, and review the analyses together to arrive at one or more conclusions. From these conclusions and using your and/or your team's professional expertise and your collective past experience as trainers, you should be able to begin the process of identifying one or more recommendations. The grouping process also facilitates the production of the summaries for the ultimate report. Writing the report is the subject of Chapter 8.

Before summarizing this chapter here is our analysis of Example 2:

Category	Times selected	%	Weighting	Weighted score
1	0	0	+2	0
2	80	57	+1	57
3	30	21	0	0
4	30	21	-1	-21
5	0	0	-2	0

TOTAL 36

Weighted Mean Score = 0.25

Summary

So to summarize this chapter, you have looked at how to make sense of the data by:

- analysing the data in a clear and simple but meaningful manner
- using the results of the analysis to identify the patterns
- sorting out what the patterns mean
- presenting the analyses in a graphic and graphical way
- grouping the analyses to identify conclusions related to the key issues raised by your customer

  and

- using the conclusions to identify recommendations.

The next step in the process is to draft the report, and this is the subject of Chapter 7.

Conclusion

This indicates that while the result is positive it is only marginally so and the narrow range points to a potential level of mediocrity which may not be acceptable within that organization.

Recommendations

One recommendation may be to develop new training which is more job related. Another could be to ensure that any new training is both interesting and fun.

Assignment:

1. *Take three segments of the data you've collected for your current TNA and present the information they yield:*

   a. *in a table*

   b. *in a graph*

   c. *in a table and graph.*

   Show the forms of presentation a, b, and c to some trusted colleagues. What do they say? Which type of presentation is most effective when it comes to communicating patterns?

2. *Using your knowledge gained from this chapter and the reaction of your colleagues to part 1 of this assignment, prepare the data for presentation in the most appropriate way.*

Write a Draft Report

In terms of hours spent on a TNA, most are already behind you when you come to writing your draft report. Without a report, your TNA is nothing. In fact, it's worse than nothing, because so many people have contributed to it that there will be a backlash of frustration and disappointment if nothing comes of it.

The report is vitally important because, together with its recommendations, it will be able to change an investigative exercise into future actions. In short, a lot depends on it.

By the time you have finished this chapter, you will be able to:

- structure a report so that it will have maximum effect
- use various techniques so that it will have maximum effect
- make authoritative recommendations
- explain what you do with your draft report and recommendations.

The Style

In most situations, the report needs to be in written form. This is the only way of ensuring its permanence and its transportability throughout your organization. So your draft, too, should be in writing.

Case Study

We asked the operations manager of a nationwide logistics company what criterion he used to decide whether or not to read a report. 'This one,' he replied, picking up a substantial booklet from his desk and weighing it in his hand. 'Too heavy', he commented, and tossed the offending document to one side.

The implications are as follows. It is not the weight of the document which is crucial. Presumably you could present the report on microfiche, were that the case. The fact is that size is usually a function of accessibility, and managers need to access information quickly or not at all. If there is any chance of the manager getting bogged down, they simply won't read it.

So you must make the body of the text accessible, and this means making it:

- clear
- brief
- clearly structured.

To achieve this, you should:

1. Use short sentences; they carry more impact than longer sentences because they convey their message more quickly and are easier to understand.

2. Use short paragraphs and make the most of the white space on the page.

3. Use bullet-points to make items on the page really stand out. It is one thing to write that laboratory staff are conscientious, highly qualified and full of ideas. It is more effective to describe them as:

   - conscientious
   - highly qualified
   - full of ideas.

4. Use headings in different types of print to identify different sections of the page. For example it is helpful for the reader to know at a glance whether they are reading about findings or recommendations.

5. Present the lists of findings in the order of importance your customer gave to the problems and aims.

Words to Avoid

There is a collection of words to avoid using anywhere in your report, and particularly in the overview. The collection includes:

- obviously
- clearly
- evidently
- naturally

. . . and the like. In our experience, people who use those and similar words are making points which are far from obvious, clear, evident or natural.

The Structure

Throughout this book I have stressed the importance of a structured approach. Producing a report is no exception. First prepare your structure.

So what should the structure of your report be?

Here list the main headings of your report in the order in which they will appear.

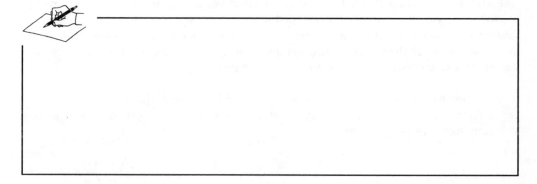

The structure of the report I'd recommend is one which appears as follows:

1. Management overview.
2. Summary of the results.
3. Recommendations linked to results.
4. Benefits of implementing the recommendations.
5. Results.
6. Appendices — including detailed methodology and raw data.

You may have more headings than the six listed here. I see these as a minimum. If you ask yourself are they necessary for the customer, and the answer is yes, then keep them. Otherwise remove them.

1.   Management Overview

Let's start with the first heading. What did you put first? Most people put the introduction first. However I'm firmly of the opinion that the first item should be an *overview* of the **Findings** and **Recommendations** — and it should be no longer than one page — at the very most, two.

There are practical reasons why this should be so. Put yourself in the position of your customer, the person who has commissioned the TNA. You know there has been some profound investigating going on, and your people have been edgy for some time. What do the people think they need? Will you be able to afford it? Can you afford not to react to what they say? What does the training function recommend? Yes, you're a mature, experienced professional, but even so, you need to know straight away what has happened — and there it is on the first page of the text. It's so much easier than flicking through pages to find it; and it's certainly much easier than summarizing the report for yourself.

Also a good overview might well capture the interest of the disinterested party and make them explore the text. Equally a bad summary might turn off an important key decision maker in your organization.

There's one final and very important point to make, and it concerns the authority of your overview. What do you think you can do to ground your overview firmly in the full report which follows it? Write your answer here.

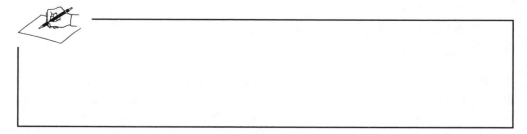

In short:

· You could cross-reference to the body of the report.

This has implications for the way you present the body of the report itself, in that there must be a way for the reader to easily identify the point you are making in the body of the report. A letter-based or numerical system of paragraph-labelling will do the trick.

2.   Summary of the Results

This section should summarize the results from each question by describing what the results mean.

When you are wondering what to include in your summary of results, you should refer back to the original brief and the topics you looked at in Chapter 6. If you were, for example, asked to collect data from various sites, then your summary should be divided geographically. If your prime aim was to obtain data from different levels of the organization's hierarchy, then your summary should reflect this structure. If your brief was to compare sites and levels in the hierarchy, then your structure should reflect this. It is sometimes helpful to present the results in grouped format by topic as on page 78 in Chapter 6.

In any case the summary should be a short description of:

- the objective
- the sample
- a very brief description of the method
- the results.

Ideally the summary should be in narrative format but it is usually appropriate to include some of the main figures in terms of averages or percentages. However, this is not the place to go into detailed description or the place to include tables and graphs. That kind of detail goes into Section 4, Results. The key aim here is to let your reader know quickly and clearly what the results are and what they mean. Work from the assumption that nothing in the data analysis is self-evident. If 'it' is there you should make it clear what 'it' is. The key throughout is to make it clear to the reader exactly what the patterns in the results mean.

3.   Recommendations Linked to Results

You will probably have a number of recommendations to make. Can you think of three features each recommendation should have to make it likely that it be acted upon? Write them here.

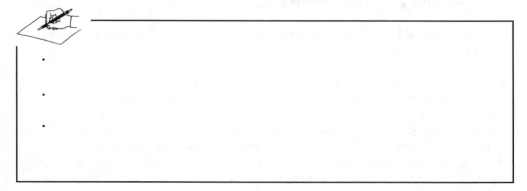

The three features recommendations need are authority, logic and acceptability.

Authority for each recommendation comes from the data you have amassed and analysed. Each recommendation should therefore be carefully cross-referenced to the rest of the information in the report. In practical terms this means that each paragraph must be marked according to an alpha or numeric system which can be quoted easily.

Logic dictates that the recommendations must appear in a workable sequence, as in a draft action plan. To pick a simple example, if you conclude that training should be cascaded down the hierarchy, then your recommendations concerning the timing and method of senior management training should appear first. Otherwise, readers will be lost.

Acceptability means that you have to take account of your organization's culture and beliefs. In some organizations you could suggest that the manager could actually do the junior's job for a week in order to experience at first-hand its complexities. In others, such a suggestion would see the report shelved indefinitely, so you should design another approach to achieving the same aim.

4.   Benefits of Implementing the Recommendations

The report you are submitting is in many respects a form of marketing exercise. Your customer/client commissioned the work, but had little idea of what the end product would be like. In short, they are not obliged to adopt your recommendations, but will adopt them if the benefits are made clear. We suggest the carrot rather than the stick.

Case Study

Bob Laxey, training manager at GKW Enterprises, identified that over 75 per cent of the production team were dissatisfied at work because they felt that they were not only unaware of what the design department was doing, they also felt that they should be consulted during the design phase of new products and that they could give the design team useful information about the capabilities and capacities of new machines.

Bob submitted his report and focused on the disadvantages of having a disaffected production team, to which senior management reacted negatively. The result was an air of conflict rather than co-operation, and this was not conducive to the implementation of change.

We maintain that a better strategy for Bob would have been to stress the advantages of co-operation between designers and producers, and the benefits to the business of addressing the production team's perceptions. You should aim to list the benefits in terms of the objectives your customer described at the outset of the process.

5.   Results

This is the section into which you put the detailed outcomes of your data analysis and where you'd include graphs and/or tables. At this stage you should go into as much detail as you need to support and justify both your summary comments and your recommendations. The structure of the results section should follow the structure of the summary section but should be numbered (or lettered) to enable the reader to find the results of any individual question.

Assuming you're happy that from a customer point of view this is the best structure, what would be the order in which you'd work to produce a report with such a structure? Write the order in which you'd work in here.

1.

2.

3.

4.

5.

The way we tend to work is in this order:

1. Results — complete all of the analysis, grouping and graph productions.
2. Summary — from 1 produce a set of summary comments.
3. Recommendations — use 1 and 2 to produce the recommendations.
4. Benefits — use 1, 2 and 3 to identify the benefits.
5. Management overview — use 1, 2, 3 and 4 to produce the overview.

Once that's done you can then add a numbering system, clarify the links between sections and confirm that all the links are made and that none of the links produces contradictory outcomes.

6. Appendices — Including Detailed Methodology and Raw Data

There only remains the final, optional step of adding any appendices you need. Into the appendices should go the fine detail of the project: for example — verbatim comments, raw data and so on. However before you spend time on this section check with your customer first to see if the information will be of any use to them. If it is not, then don't include it.

Here you include all the raw data you collected. If there is simply too much to include, then you must indicate:

· where the raw data is being stored

· how long it will be kept.

Finally, this draft report must be submitted to the client who will then sign it off. The chances are the final report will need to be presented in a more glossy, attractive format, and that there will be several copies of it produced. You cannot afford to invest time and money in the reproduction process if the client is going to ask you to change anything. (The nature of these changes we will discuss in Chapter 8). Similarly, digests of the TNA may be distributed on a large scale to all employees in the business, and it is crucial that a consistent message comes across. So wait until your client confirms, in writing, that what you are saying is not only right, but expressed in an acceptable way.

Summary

This chapter has shown you how to prepare a draft report. There are six sections to a successful TNA report:

1. Management overview.
2. Summary of the results.
3. Recommendations linked to the results.
4. Benefits of implementing the recommendations.
5. Results.
6. Appendices — including detailed methodology and raw data.

The key to its success is threefold. It must be:

- clear
- brief
- authoritative.

Your recommendations should moreover be relevant to the culture of the organization.

Finally in this chapter you saw how important it is that your client should confirm acceptance of your report in writing before you begin to produce copies and digests.

Assignment:

1. *Lay out the report of your current TNA using the headings given above. Make sure that you keep one copy for yourself before presenting the report to your customer.*

2. *Compare the layout of the current report with previous reports you may have filed. How would you have improved your previous reports? Discuss your findings with members of your team who help you to prepare and compile reports.*

Produce and Distribute a Final Report and Recommendations

By this stage in the TNA there are only one or two issues outstanding. It is possible that your draft report has been accepted and approved wholesale, in which case you will only have to deal with distribution and presentation matters. But you may find yourself in negotiation with your client about what is included in your final report, in which case there is a little extra work to do. By the time you have finished this chapter, you will be able to:

- state what is and what is not negotiable in your final report
- deal with key distribution questions
- plan the final presentation of your report.

Negotiable vs Non-negotiable

You have submitted your draft report, and your customer calls you. There are 'one or two things' he or she would like to go over.

On which items in your TNA are you not prepared to give ground? Write your answer here.

The only non-negotiable items are the raw data. You cannot pretend either that you never asked such-and-such a question, or that the people didn't answer it in the way they did. You see, it's not a secret; the people themselves know what you've been asking and why, and if all reference to it disappears or is distorted, someone will want to know why. Everything else is negotiable:

- the way you have presented your findings
- the emphasis you have placed on certain items
- the courses of action you have recommended provided that the integrity of your conclusions remains intact.

Distribution Questions

The distribution of the results of the TNA and the recommendations is itself a project within a project, and you will need to apply the OCSER criteria identified in Chapter 5, namely:

- objectives
- correct sequence
- start date
- end date
- resources.

The objectives, if they are specific, will take account of such matters as:

- how many versions of the report will there be?
- how will you assess the presentation style to make it appropriate to its audience?
- how many copies will you need to produce?

Once you have the answers to these questions, you will be in a better position to consider the sequencing, the resource implications, and the start and end dates.

The Final Presentation

We said earlier that your report may have to be presented to a group of people rather than merely delivered in a plain envelope. If this is to happen with your TNA, there are a number of points you must bear in mind:

- do I or my team have presentation skills?
- do we have the resources to produce:
  — overhead projector acetates?
  — handouts; perhaps copies or extracts from the report?
  — slides?
- how much time will it take to prepare a presentation, bearing in mind the need to:
  — confirm with your customer the main point to bring out?
  — distil the main points?
  — design your presentation programme?
  — rehearse?
  — produce visual aids and papers?
- when is the presentation scheduled?
- will you need any special equipment?
- are there any special considerations? You might like to include:
  — taped interviews with respondents
  — video footage of working arrangements.

As a final point, we advise you that the best presentations allow a reasonable amount of time for the audience to ask questions of the presenter. Since you have been methodical in all your processes throughout the TNA, this questioning should hold no terrors for you. Because you have designed and planned it carefully, and justified your actions to yourself and your customer at every stage, you can confidently expect to have an answer for every question, but if your customer can give you any prior information about the audience's special interests, so much the better. You can certainly expect detailed questions on what your recommendations are going to cost.

Summary

Chapter 8 has shown you first of all that your raw data and the questions you asked are not up for negotiation with your customer at the report stage. Your recommendations and proposals clearly are negotiable, and you may have to make some changes to cater to your customer's needs.

You saw that the production of the final report should be run like a mini-project, because you will find yourself balancing your resources against the demands of the customer's schedule. Moreover there may be different versions of the final report for different audiences.

Finally you studied a list of questions which you must take into account if you have to prepare a presentation in support of your agreed proposals.

Assignment:

Use this checklist to prepare a presentation:

Aims and objectives of presentation identified.

Best people to do the presentation identified.

Venue arranged.

Timing arranged.

Audience specified and invited.

Script prepared.

Visual aids prepared.

Handouts prepared.

Rehearsals.

Preparation for questioning session complete.

Budgetary analysis complete.

Conclusion

By sorting out your TNA in a structured way, you will achieve the following:

- cost-effective working — with little or no time wasted on asking irrelevant questions, and a rapid production process for materials

- precisely targeted questions, completely in line with the organization's needs and the needs of your customer

- good working relations with all involved — sound co-operation with everyone

- efficient collection of ample, accurate and relevant data in a usable form

- a clear, understandable analysis of what the data mean in terms of action to be taken

- a concise, persuasive report designed to set in motion a series of actions to help the organization achieve its mission.

All this we have demonstrated. We wish you well with your future analyses.